Echoes Of Unfelt

emotions | feelings | thoughts

Kumar Patel

BookLeaf Publishing

India | USA | UK

Copyright © Kumar Patel

All Rights Reserved.

This book has been self-published with all reasonable efforts taken to make the material error-free by the author. No part of this book shall be used, reproduced in any manner whatsoever without written permission from the author, except in the case of brief quotations embodied in critical articles and reviews.

The Author of this book is solely responsible and liable for its content including but not limited to the views, representations, descriptions, statements, information, opinions, and references ["Content"]. The Content of this book shall not constitute or be construed or deemed to reflect the opinion or expression of the Publisher or Editor. Neither the Publisher nor Editor endorse or approve the Content of this book or guarantee the reliability, accuracy, or completeness of the Content published herein and do not make any representations or warranties of any kind, express or implied, including but not limited to the implied warranties of merchantability, fitness for a particular purpose.

The Publisher and Editor shall not be liable whatsoever...

Made with ❤ on the BookLeaf Publishing Platform

www.bookleafpub.in

www.bookleafpub.com

Dedication

To the quiet hearts,

The ones who feel everything but say nothing, who hide their storms behind smiles and carry their struggles in silence. This is for you—the ones who are still figuring out how to speak up, still trying to make sense of all the feelings that seem too big for words.

I hope these words might answer some of your inner thoughts or help you let out what you've been holding in. May you find comfort here, in knowing that you are not the only one who feels too much and says too little. You are seen. You are heard. You are not alone.

Preface

Some feelings never make it past the heart—they stay hidden, too raw, too sacred, too unsure of how they'd sound if spoken aloud.

This book is for those unspoken emotions.
For the questions you ask in silence, for the storms that never show on your face, for the weight you carry in your chest but never name.

Each poem is a whisper from the soul—mine, yours, or perhaps someone you've never met.
A voice borrowed from hundreds of hearts, stitched together in verses that might echo your own thoughts, your own fears, your own quiet hopes.

This isn't just a collection of poems.
It's a mirror of the emotions we often don't speak, a diary of unnoticed moments, a rollercoaster of everything we feel but struggle to explain.

This journey unfolds in three phases:
Phase 1 — *Questions of Life (Unsaid Doubts & Identity Crises):*
Here, the poems explore the self — the aching

search for purpose, the uncertainty of growth, the rawness of fear, and the fragile, ever-changing nature of identity.

Phase 2 — *Whispers of Living (Bonds, Moments, and Fleeting Connections)*:

Poems that drift through the breeze of life — situationships, friendships, memories, firsts, thoughts of perfection,   and the silent bonds we form without realizing.

Phase 3 — *The Rise and Fall of Love (From Bloom to Ruin)*:

The most intimate phase, where love blooms and heartbreak devastates. Where emotions are at their highest, and the fall is even harder. It is about giving, breaking, losing, and yet somehow, still surviving.

Let these words sit with you.

Let them answer questions you didn't know you were asking.
And if even one line feels like home, then this book has already found its voice in you.

Acknowledgements

To my **dear friends**—thank you for being my anchors. Your support has been my strength, your belief my motivation. In moments of doubt, you reminded me to keep writing. Your constant encouragement and thoughtful feedback helped me grow with every word I wrote. You saw something in me even when I couldn't, and for that, I am endlessly grateful.

A heartfelt thanks to those **kind souls** who, knowingly or unknowingly, contributed to the birth of this book—through conversations, shared emotions, or even a passing thought that sparked an idea. You may never realize the role you played, but your presence made a difference. Some of you offered a word, a silence, a smile —little things that echoed in my heart and found their way into these pages.

To the ones who stayed during the quiet phases, who didn't ask for explanations but simply offered their presence—thank you. Your silent companionship held me steady when words refused to come.

To the voices I've heard in passing, the strangers whose stories left imprints, and the fleeting moments that

bloomed into poetry—thank you for inspiring me
without even knowing it.

To the late nights, to the chaos of emotions, to the
moments of raw vulnerability—thank you for shaping
this book into something real. This is not just ink on
paper—it is breath, ache, hope, and healing. It is
everything I never said, finally finding a voice.

And finally, to you, the reader—thank you for holding
this book in your hands, for opening your heart to these
unspoken pieces of mine. May you find echoes of your
own feelings in these pages. May they comfort you,
move you, or simply remind you that you are not alone.

This book is as much yours as it is mine.
Thank you for walking beside me through this journey of
unspoken feelings and silent poetry.

1. CHOCKED

In the drop of distress, where shadows loom,
I find myself trapped in a somber tomb.
With words caught in my throat, I gasp for air,
As if life's essence slips away, unfair.

I can't breathe anymore, feels like dying,
A symphony of pain, my soul is crying.
Metaphors dance upon my weakened lungs,
An orchestra of sorrow, where anguish stuns.

My heart, a heavy stone, burdened with strife,
Crushed by the weight of this unending life.
Personification lends voice to my fears,
As silence suffocates, drowning in tears.

The world spins around, a cruel carousel,
Each breath a reminder of an earthly spell.
Similes paint a picture of my distress,
Like a wounded bird, robbed of its nest.

Every inhalation, a battle for breath,
An ode to suffocation, embracing death.

Hyperbole amplifies my inner scream,
Asphyxiated dreams, a shattered gleam.

In this maze of pain, I search for light,
A metaphorical respite from this fight.
But the air grows thinner, hope slips away,
Metonymy binds my spirit, in dismay.

I can't breathe anymore, feels like dying,
As personified pain leaves me sighing.
Figures of speech, my only solace found,
Expressing the suffocation, profound.

Yet within this darkness, a flicker burns bright,
A metaphorical ember, a glimmer of light.
With perseverance, I'll rise from despair's grip,
Metaphors may falter, but my spirit won't slip.

2. Life Entangled

What if you never figure it all out?
You don't have to.
Life isn't a test you're failing—
it's a road you're still learning to walk.

Who are you?
You're a soul in progress,
not a product with a label.
You are not the roles they gave you—
you are the stories you survive.

Why are you here?
To feel.
To lose and still choose love.
To fall and still get up.
To be human—raw, messy, real.
You're here because this world needed *you*,
not a version of you—*you*.

What is it all for?
Not for perfect grades or applause.
Not for proving yourself every second.
It's for the quiet joy in small mornings,
for holding someone's hand without needing words.

It's for those sacred moments
where you finally feel seen.

And when you ask—
Am I even worth anything?
Let me say this with all the truth in me:
Yes. You are.
Not because of what you do.
Not because you shine every day.
But because even when you're shattered,
you still try to give love.
Because even tired eyes still carry dreams.

Some days you won't feel motivated.
That's not failure—it's fatigue.
Rest is not quitting.
Pause is not weakness.
You're allowed to not have it all together.
That's what makes you whole.

You think of giving up?
But there are pages you haven't lived yet,
people who haven't met your soul,
moments waiting to be *your favorite memory*.
Don't cut the story short—
you're still in the rising action.

The answers won't always come in thunder.
Sometimes, they arrive as
laughter with the right people,
a late-night song that understands you,
a quiet "me too" from someone who gets it.

Give life time.
Give *yourself* time.
You're not behind—
you're blooming at your own pace.

Even tangled lives can unravel.
Even lost hearts can find home.
And even if no one claps when you rise,
rise anyway.
Because this life, this fight,
this *you*—
is still worth it.

3. Where I Begin

They never told me the hardest part
Wouldn't be walking—it'd be where to start.
Two paths stood still, calling my name,
One wrapped in love, one wrapped in flame.
The first wore faces I'd always known,
With roots so deep, they felt like home.

Their dreams were stitched inside my skin—
"You're meant for this," they said with grin.
The other? Quieter. It looked like *me,*
Worn-out shoes, a heart half-free.
It didn't promise ease or grace,
Just the chance to find my place.

One road would keep the house lights warm,
A steady hand through every storm.
The other road might leave me cold—
But carried stories yet untold.

I stood in silence. I heard them both—
The call of duty, the rebel's oath.
And deep inside, my soul confessed:
"I don't know which one fits me best."

What if I chased what I adore,
And left my loved ones wanting more?
But what if staying left me numb,
A song unsung, a voice gone dumb?

So here's the truth they never teach—
Not every dream is out of reach.
But timing, child, is what defines
Which dream to hold… and which one finds.

You can walk their way and still be whole,
Then slowly climb your mountain goal.
Sacrifice doesn't mean goodbye—
It just means *some dreams take more sky.*

And yes, you'll lose some things you crave,
To keep the bonds you choose to save.
But what survives beyond the test—
Is what your heart will love the best.
So let time guide, don't rush the end.
Be your own compass, not just a friend.

Both roads are valid. Let them be—
The one you walk will shape your *"me."*
You're not just here to choose or prove.
You're here to *live*, to grow, to move.

And when you're asked, "Which path was true?"
Say, "The one that let me stay me too."

4. In the Quiet After You

You came into my life like a soft season,
quietly, gently, the way breath moves—
unnoticed, but essential.
You weren't loud or rushed, just there,
a presence that felt like something I'd been waiting for
without knowing I was missing it.
I never knew strangers could feel so familiar.
You didn't ask for permission—
you simply made a place for yourself,
in my stories and my silences,
in the dreams I hadn't spoken aloud,
in the wounds I had never dared to heal.
You made me feel seen,
heard,
held—
in ways I didn't know I could be.

And for a while, everything made sense.
Laughter tasted like home,
sunsets promised me a future
where we could always be this way.
Even silence, when it sat between us,
was warm and comforting,
like it belonged to us,

a language we spoke without words.

But then you left.
Not in a way that makes noise,
but in a silence that echoed louder
than the harshest of words.
One day you were here,
and the next,
I was mourning someone
who was still alive but out of reach.
That's the worst kind of loss,
isn't it?
When the person you need is still breathing,
but their presence is as distant as a dream
you never get to wake up from.

I begged the universe for some kind of sign,
for a reason,
for anything that could make sense
of something that never should've ended.
But all I got was stillness—
a quiet that lingered
long after you were gone.

And through the silence,
I realized that not everyone who feels like home
is meant to stay.

Some people are storms dressed in comfort,
meant to teach you how deeply you can feel,
how easily you can break,
and how strong you are for surviving it.

Some people were never meant to love you—
they were lessons in disguise,
lessons that burn and sting
but leave behind the truth:
Not every bond is built to last,
not every heart is meant to hold yours.
Some people are just passing through,
leaving behind only ache,
and clarity.

They taught me to be careful
who I give my soul to,
who I trust with my vulnerability.
They taught me that not everyone is worth it,
that it's okay to listen to my intuition
and not just my heart.

And maybe, they had to leave
so I would stop shrinking to fit inside their absence,
so I would stop chasing pain
and start understanding that presence
isn't always peace.

So now, here I am,
with nothing but memories—
but memories don't fade.
They stay,
etched in time,
alive even after the person has gone.

So I'll hold them,
but I won't chase them.
I'll love what was,
mourn what couldn't be,
and let that be enough.

The next time someone feels like home,
I'll make sure their foundation is strong,
that they're here to stay
and not just visit.
Because I'm worth more than people who leave quietly—
more than a lesson wrapped in goodbye.

I deserve someone who stays,
who isn't afraid to hold my heart
when the storm comes.
Until they arrive,
I'll let this heartbreak soften me,
not shrink me.

5. Silent Inheritance

Life's most certain, silent guest
Is not the love we chase or rest—
But that old cloak we're made to wear,
The weight of what we ought to bear.

It shows up dressed in many skins—
In school report cards, violin strings,
In buttoned shirts and bowed-down heads,
In dreams we wear that aren't our threads.

Sometimes it walks in parents' eyes,
In future plans and lullabies.
It hides in words like *"Make us proud"*,
And smiles that only praise the loud.

It drapes itself on every child,
In homes both quiet and homes run wild.
No hand escapes, no soul walks free
From what the world expects to see.
They shape us early, soft with praise,
Then harden us in hidden ways.
A father's pride, a mother's name—
A thousand dreams that aren't the same.

We smile to earn, we bow to stay,
We kneel to make their sky less grey.
And though the heart may beat its truth,
It learns to dim the songs of youth.

Not once are we quite asked aloud
If we would trade the cheers or crowd
For something small, but deeply ours—
A peace not built on borrowed hours.

Some learn to carry it with grace,
While some collapse beneath its face.
And few are told, in whispered tone,
"You're not a failure to want your own."

But here's the ache: we still hold tight—
To duty dressed as what feels right.
We miss our turns, we miss the sun,
All while becoming someone's "someone."

Yet even there, beneath the strain,
The soul still hums through silent pain.
It waits for nights when no one speaks—
To ask itself what *it* still seeks.

And if we're brave—and few are so—
We learn to let those questions grow.

We learn that dreams don't have to die
To keep the stars in someone's sky.

Yes, we were made to bear their hopes,
But we can climb our own small slopes.
And maybe not all loves will cheer,
But truth will make its echo clear.

So wear the weight, but check the seam—
Make room for both: their dream, *and* dream.
Live kindly—but don't disappear.
You, too, are meant to matter here.

6. Untranslated

I said it, again and again—
in words, in sighs,
in the way my eyes begged for someone to stay long
enough
to hear what I wasn't strong enough to scream.

They nodded.
They smiled.
They misunderstood.

They heard the noise of my voice,
but never the meaning.
They saw the cracks,
and called them moods.

They called my silence stubborn.
They called my sadness ungrateful.
They called my distance rebellion.
They called my breaking selfish.

But no one—
not even once—
asked what it cost me to keep showing up in pieces.

I started shrinking inside my own skin,
folding my dreams into smaller, quieter shapes—
until even I forgot
what they looked like unfolded.

Parents loved the child they wanted me to be.
Friends loved the laughs, not the loneliness.
Lovers loved the illusion, not the exhaustion.

Nobody loved the parts that were hard to understand.

And slowly, painfully,
I learned:

The world does not slow down to hear your heart break.
It claps for your survival
but never asks what you buried to stay alive.

You reach for comfort—
they hand you conditions.
You reach for truth—
they hand you noise.

And somewhere between all the reaching
and all the losing,
you stop.

Not out of anger.
Not even out of sadness.
Out of knowing.

Knowing that some aches will outlive the need for
apology.
Some wounds will whisper for the rest of your life.
And some stories were never meant
to be understood by the ones you loved.

So you carry your unsaid things like old songs,
like fading photographs,
like ghosts you dare not speak to anymore.

You stop asking for ears that cannot hear you.
You stop building bridges that always burn.

And you let the loneliness
settle in your bones
like a second kind of blood.

Because maybe—
maybe being misunderstood
was never the curse.
Maybe hoping they would understand
was.

7. The Quiet Collapse

"You're so happy all the time," they believe.
And we nod,
like good puppets,
strings tied to expectations we never asked for.

We sit in crowded rooms,
smiling at jokes we don't hear,
drinking coffee we don't taste,
celebrating days we don't want to live.

We become experts—
at faking excitement,
at hiding the exhaustion,
at pretending we aren't breaking in places
no one will ever think to look.

Because honesty makes people uncomfortable.
Because pain is only palatable when it's poetic.
Because no one stays long for ugly truths.

And so—
we tuck our sadness under polite laughter,
we swallow our screams with second cups of coffee,
we bury the truth in "maybe tomorrow will be better."

But when the door clicks shut,
when the mirror meets our gaze,
when the night strips us bare—
the mask peels off.

And all that's left
is the unbearable,
unchangeable truth:

We are not okay.
We are tired of pretending.
We are tired of surviving.
We are tired of hoping someone will notice the tremble
in our smiles.

And maybe the worst part is—
even we forget who we are
without the mask.

Because somewhere between the pretending and the
surviving,
we buried the real us —
so deep,
so forgotten,
even if someone tried to find us now,
there would be nothing left to save.

8. Situationships

In the depths of a delicate dance we tread,
Caught in a web of emotions, tangled thread.
A situationship, a delicate affair,
Neither here nor there, but existing in the air.

We tiptoe along the blurred lines we've drawn,
Unsure of where we stand, like a fleeting dawn.
Moments shared, like stolen fragments of time,
A love that's undefined, a rhythm out of rhyme.

We revel in the sparks that ignite our souls,
Yet fear the flames that could consume us whole.
Bound by unspoken rules, we cautiously sway,
In this uncharted gray, where hearts may stray.

In this limbo we exist, suspended in space,
Navigating the intricacies of our embrace.
A situationship, where hope and doubt collide,
A rollercoaster ride, our hearts cannot hide.

But amidst the uncertainty that surrounds,
There's a beauty in the moments we have found.
For in this fragile connection we have grown,
A bond uniquely our own, a love yet unknown.

So let us embrace this transient affair,
For we are here, in the now, aware.
In this situationship, we'll tread with grace,
Finding solace in this delicate embrace

9. Breeze

In the gentle breeze, life whispers its tale,
A delicate dance of joy and travail.
It teaches us to flow, to sway and bend,
To embrace the unknown, and to transcend.

Like the breeze, life moves with ebb and flow,
Carrying us forward, to places we don't know.
Sometimes gentle and soothing, a soft caress,
Other times fierce and wild, a storm to address.

It whispers of resilience, in moments of despair,
Reminding us to rise, to breathe in the air.
To find solace in movement, in letting go,
And to embrace the winds, wherever they may blow.

The breeze teaches us the art of being free,
To let go of attachments, to simply be.
To dance with grace, and to surrender,
To the rhythm of life, in its endless splendor.

So let us embrace the breeze, as it guides our way,
Living each moment, in the present, we stay.
For in its whispers, we find strength to strive,
To live life fully, and to truly thrive.

10. A Bond- They Don't Write Enough About

There are friendships that don't need noise to be heard,
where an empty voice note
is enough to know—
you're hurting.

Friendships where words are clumsy,
but eye contact says everything.

Where your smallest wins
are celebrated louder than your own voice would dare,
and your ugliest days
are met with arms wide enough to hold the storms you
can't name.

A bond stitched not by circumstance,
nor blood,
nor fleeting seasons—
but by something quieter, stronger:
an unspoken promise to stay.
To stand.
To carry.

The kind of friendship where trust isn't asked for—

it's woven into every glance, every laugh, every furious
defense in your absence.
Where you could be drowning in your own failures,
and still, they'd be the first to throw you a rope
and remind you of every reason you are not your
downfall.

A friendship where their growth feels like your own
victory,
where jealousy has no soil to grow,
because you've only ever wanted to see them fly higher,
even if your own wings are tired.

The world looks at you both—
a boy and a girl,
or two souls too synced to separate—
and they whisper,
There's no way it's just friendship.

But it is.
It's friendship,
in its purest, fiercest, most fearless form.
It's the late-night phone calls,
the 3AM memes,
the hand squeezing yours when words would only
cheapen the ache.

It's finding someone who believes in your dreams louder
than you do,
someone who sees every flaw, every crack—
and calls it beautiful anyway.

It's the way they fight for your light
when all you see is dark.

It's friendship,
the kind poets forget to write about
because they think only love stories deserve songs.

But I know better.

I know *this*—
this million-dollar smile,
this laughter built like cathedrals,
this fortress of loyalty and late-night "you'll be okay"
texts—
this is the miracle we spend lifetimes looking for.

Not lovers.
Not saviors.
But the rare few who see you,
stand with you,
and stay—
no matter what storms you drag through their front

door.

Some friendships are made of gold,
some of blood,
but the rarest ones—
the rarest ones
are made of soul.

11. Firsts

One day, she'll take her very first step,
Tiny feet wobbling — and I'll forget to catch my breath.
From the moment she says "Dada" with a grin so wide,
To the first time she runs — I'll be right by her side.

We'll go on dates, just her and me,
Cartoons one day, thrillers the next — wild and free.
She'll laugh at the silliest things on screen,
And I'll laugh harder — just watching her beam.

Her first drawing will be a sky turned pink,
And I'll hang it up — it's perfect, more than she'd think.
Her first school day, I'll wave with a tear,
Hiding my fear, smiling so she won't see it's me who's scared here.

Her first crush? I'll notice it all,
The way she hums a song or smiles at a text call.
I won't tease her — just listen, just stay,
Maybe slip a joke, then quietly pray.

Her first love... oh, I'll try not to show,
That it scares me a little, but I'll let her grow.
I'll be the calm when her world spins fast,

Knowing not every "forever" is meant to last.

And when her heart breaks — as first loves do,
I'll be there with ice cream... and tissues too.
But more than that, with arms open wide,
To remind her she's never unloved — not while I'm alive.

Through all her "firsts," I won't just be near,
I'll be her shadow, her shelter, her silent cheer.
Not to hold her back, but to help her fly,
To be her strength when she just wants to cry.

She won't need to search for someone to care,
She'll know — Dad was always there.
From first steps, to first falls, to every twist,
This is the story of a father...
And all her firsts.

12. Perfection- A Myth

We chase perfection, like a shadow that never stays,
Clutching at something that always slips away.
We try to make our lives a flawless lie,
But each step forward only makes us ask why.

We look at others, through eyes blurred by need,
Searching for a reflection, for a life we don't heed.
We want to be flawless — perfect in every way,
But it's only in the cracks that we truly find our way.

In the quiet of our minds, we hear the call:
"To be something more, to be nothing at all."
We build our lives on fragile dreams,
Hoping to live up to the impossible schemes.

We hide our flaws like sins in the dark,
Afraid that our imperfection will leave a mark.
But no matter how much we hide the truth,
It's the flaws that define us, from age to youth.

We wear our smiles like painted masks,
Hiding the emptiness behind every task.
We think perfection is the answer we crave,
But it's only a prison, a shallow grave.

And when we fail — as we always do —
We stare at the pieces, wondering who we are through.
How did we become so lost in the chase,
That we forgot the real beauty, the real grace?

The truth is painful, the truth is clear,
Perfection is a lie we tell ourselves year after year.
It's a cage built from expectations and fear,
A cage so tight we can't breathe, can't hear.

We think perfection is the answer we seek,
But it's the imperfections that make us unique.
It's in the brokenness we truly grow,
In the shattered pieces, we begin to know.

So we stand, in the ruins of our desires,
Trying to ignite perfection's never-ending fires.
But the truth is dark, and it cuts like a knife:
The only perfection is the imperfection of life.

And in the quiet, we finally see,
Perfection wasn't meant to be.
It's in the flaws, the cracks, the scars —
That we find our true self, no matter how far.

13. Stillness

When the day is done and the night slips down.
And I've turned my back on the busy town.
And come once more to welcome gate
Where roses are red and so are my hands.

When day is done and I've come once more
To my quiet street and the friendly door.
I throw my coat on a near-by chair
And say farewell to my pack of care.

When the day is done, all the hurt and strife
And the selfishness and the greed of life.
Are left behind in the busy town;

In shadows deep, where despair resides,
A solemn whisper, where hope subsides.
A heart burdened, with burdens untold,
A tale of darkness, yearning to unfold.

Willing to die, echoes softly heard,
A cry for respite, a soul's whispered word.
But in the depths of this darkest plea,
May strength arise, like a phoenix set free.

For beneath the weight of sorrow's strain,
Lies resilience's spark, a flickering flame.
In the depths of pain, where courage lies,
A spirit awakens, prepared to rise.

Though darkness blinds and burdens weigh,
A glimmer of light can lead the way.
The depths of despair can hold us tight,
But a will to survive can ignite.

Hold on, dear soul, in the face of despair,
For life's vast tapestry is yours to wear.
Embrace the struggles, for in every trial,
Strength and resilience find their revival.

Amidst the shadows, a flicker of hope,
In the darkest moments, new depths we cope.
Remember, dear one, there's love to find,
Hold onto life, for it's one of a kind.

14. Thoughts - The Battle Within

Lost in the labyrinth I built in my mind,
Worn hands trace walls I can never unwind.
A prisoner of thoughts, I battle and bleed,
Fighting wars no one can hear or see.

Shadows of choices claw at my chest,
Every "what if" screaming louder than the rest.
Which path, which face, which lie to believe?
A thousand selves — none I can retrieve.

Hope flickers, thin as a dying breath,
 While despair hums soft hymns of death.
I am the war, I am the sword,
I am the broken prayer, unheard.

In the pit of indecision I sink and sway,
Where every tomorrow just slips away.
I crave escape from the voice in my head —
Yet even silence screams louder instead.

Inside this chaos, a bitter truth is sewn:
You are your own cage, your own cornerstone.
No map will come, no savior will call —

Only the pieces you stitch as you fall.

So let me fall, let me crack, let me break,
 Till from these ruins, something real will wake.
 A self not polished, but battered and true,
 Forged from every battle I didn't mean to lose.

A version of me, stitched with bruises and screws.
No longer a soul that dreams of the light,
 But a body that survives, night after night.

My ribs are shelves of memories decayed,
Each breath I take, a debt never repaid.
In the hollows of my chest, the winds of regret,
Howl lullabies I'll never forget.

The mirror no longer flinches at my face,
It knows this wreckage, this hollowed space.
I do not search for beauty anymore —
Only reasons to fight, only reasons to endure.

In this endless waltz of silence and screams,
I dance with the ghosts of my abandoned dreams.
Their cold hands cling to the curve of my spine,
Whispering of failures I tried to define.

If there is salvation, it does not come sweet,

It comes dragging, clawing, through broken feet.
It is not a sunrise — it's a crack in the wall,
It is not soaring — it's learning to crawl.

I do not pray for the storm to cease,
I pray for the strength to drown in peace.
And if tomorrow demands another war,
I'll fight — even if I don't know what for.

Because somewhere, deep in the marrow of pain,
There is a savage kind of strength to gain.
Not the strength to smile, not to pretend —
But the strength to live...
When you wish it would end.

15. SHE

Why is her voice so addictive?
Melodious, soft, yet sharp like wine —
it soothes my broken, battered soul,
and makes even my darkest demons resign.

The world may spin in frantic race,
but with her, time forgets to breathe.
When we talk, my fears dissolve —
they sleep beneath her whispered wreath.

She is a home —
not a place, but a feeling —
a haven stitched from soft serenity.
While chaos rages beyond my walls,
her calm cradles me in quiet divinity.

Her words —
a lullaby stitched in the seams of dusk,
singing me into places where pain cannot follow.
Her voice —
a symphony laced in secret sorrow,
making my heart tremble and hollow.

Why is her voice so addictive?

Each syllable like a spell unwinds,
I drift deeper into her trance,
lost between her pauses, lost between her sighs.

I could listen for lifetimes,
each hour folding into the next unseen;
her voice — my only compass,
leading me through nightmares, into forgotten dreams.

It dances through my broken places,
a golden thread across the dark,
each word a tender shiver,
rekindling a long-dead spark.

In twilight's hush, her laughter spills —
a fragile balm against despair,
an echo of promises she may not say,
but somehow, I know she'll care.

Why is her voice so addictive?
Because in its warmth, I find my way —
a path through every ruined thing,
where broken souls still choose to stay.

16. A Diary of Two Strangers, One Heart

I turned twenty-one, the candles were lit,
Among the gifts, one quietly chose to sit.
An old diary, wrapped in silk and grace,
Her handwriting dancing on every page.

She was my grandmother — the melody, the song,
And he, my grandfather — discipline, strict, strong.
Their marriage was arranged, two unknown names,
Two different worlds playing destiny's games.

He lived by rules, sharp as a knife,
While she painted her soul into notes of life.
He rose with the sun, a soldier of routine,
She dreamt with the moon, soft, serene.

They barely spoke in the early days,
He frowned at flaws, she sang through the haze.
Once, just a pinch of salt too less,
He hurled the plate in cold distress.

Yet she stayed, with warmth in her eyes,
Trying to read the storms behind his sighs.
He built his empire, brick by brick,

But joy was something he couldn't quite pick.

She sang her heart in studios unknown,
While he chased gold, alone, alone.
And just when he turned to give her his time,
She stepped away from dreams — made his hers, made him shine.

They bloomed in silence, slowly, deep,
Raised children, shared laughs, and tears to weep.
Weekends, he cooked — clumsy but proud,
Their love no longer needed to be loud.

He'd take the grandkids to movies and plays,
She'd hum soft lullabies on lazy Sundays.
And one night, while her favorite tune softly played,
She slipped away in sleep, like a fading cascade.

He didn't cry. He simply froze.
Became the man he was once — composed.
He gave his empire to his children's name,
But he himself was never quite the same.

Never slept in their bed again,
Only on the sofa, with memories and pain.
Each day, he'd speak to her photograph alone,
Argue, smile, or just sit like stone.

Until today... I opened that book,
And the whole world around me shook.
Poems, letters — stories untold,
Of the fire and the frost, the young and the old.

Two strangers who became each other's soul,
Two halves that somehow made one whole.
Each page was soaked in unsaid tears,
In lullabies, fears, and passing years.

And I watched him, as he found it too,
The diary — her gift that finally broke through.
For once, he cried, but not in pain —
He whispered her name again and again.

Now, he still talks to her every day,
Only now, her words talk back, in a different way.
And I, the grandson, hold their past in my hand...
Two strangers, one love — a story unplanned.

17. When Two Givers Stay Quiet

She wants love.
But not the noisy kind.
Not fireworks or grand declarations —
just someone who sees her,
even in her quietest ache,
and stays.

He stays.
But he isn't sure if what he feels
is love —
or just that gravity
that makes someone feel different
without knowing why.

She craves a hug
but stops herself.
She wants to whisper, *"I need someone."*
But bites her tongue.
Because her heart has been a battlefield once,
and she refuses to go to war again
for a maybe.

He listens when she talks about her day,

remembers the little things she forgot she shared,
laughs at her sarcasm like it's a melody
he didn't know he needed.

He doesn't say, *I love you.*
He says,
"Did you eat?"
"Get home safe."
"Call me when you can."

She is the kind of strong
that's built from heartbreak.
She gave once —
too much, too soon —
to people who didn't stay.
Now, she gives in silence.
In soft smiles, in holding back.
She calls it survival.

He, meanwhile,
tries to understand why her voice
makes the world slow down,
why he wants to fix the sadness in her eyes
without ever asking her to change.

Every night,
he stays up on calls longer than he should,

but still doesn't want to say goodbye.

They don't call this love.
They call it friendship.
They call it *something special.*
They call it *connection.*
But in the cracks between their words,
a quiet storm is brewing.

Two givers —
standing face to face,
holding all they have,
too scared to hand it over.

He gives because he hopes.
She holds back because she's afraid of losing herself.

He looks for signs.
She hides them.

He would give her everything
if only he knew what she needed.
But she won't ask.
Because she's tired of giving
and ending up empty.

Still —

they orbit.
Two versions of the same longing
trapped in different bodies,
writing a story without ink,
without pages,
without names.

Is it love?
They won't ask.
They'll just wait —
for a miracle
neither believes in
but both secretly want.

And that's the heartbreak —
that two hearts,
so full,
 so ready,
so right for each other,
stay silent
because silence feels safer
than wanting more.

This isn't a relationship.
This isn't just friendship.
It's something suspended
between holding on

and letting go.

Maybe one day,
they'll say what they feel.
Or maybe they'll just stay —
giving, aching,
quietly building a love story
the world will never hear.

18. The Last Goodbye

Was standing alone, looking at the moon's eerie glow,
Breeze touching my soul, whispers of a love unknown.
In the shadows we danced, a passion forbidden to show.

Quite lovely it was, but yet I felt lonely,
Deep down, we both knew who was guilty.
Your eyes had a story that remained untold,
I was running the other side, but still kept searching for you.

Torn between self-blame and a hidden truth,
In the echoes of night, regrets take root.
Yet I still search for those eyes, those memories,
Lost in a labyrinth of love's shattered reveries.

I guess we came so far with nothing,
I believed in the love which was from me only.
The light of the moon reminds me of the tears,
I still want to shout but no one to hear.

The scars you carved, they left me broken,
A heart once whole, now words unspoken.
Shaken, unsteady, I stumbled in despair,
A soul in turmoil, lost in the air.

Haunted by echoes of promises untrue,
I walked a path where love withdrew.
In the ruins of what we used to be,

Never wanna run to those paths again,
I am afraid to be left broken again.
My blurred vision is almost permanent now,
I am tired, restless, forgetting my old self,
Why does this wind send chills now?

No self-blame, but I questioned my part,
Trapped in your web, a victim of your art.
Loved ones warned, yet I fell in your spell,
Now you rest in peace, and others dwell.

In grief and heartache, shattered they stand,
While you lie in the coffin, a life in your hand.

Now you're gone, memories alone remain,
I'm left with a heart forever stained.
To love again, I'll never find the way.

So let me close the chapter,
A big part of me.
I loved you with all my heart,
But that wasn't it.

You chose to betray the unconditional love.

 I was left with no other option but that.
Thanks for the wine you had last night,
I still love you, but I'm scared of what the world will
think.
So quietly, I buried you, but remember your sin.
I forgive you now because you accepted it at last.
So I offer you deep sleep, and I hope you never come
back.

I struggle to escape your lingering signs,
Amidst grieving souls, solace hardly aligns.
 They weep and lament, yet absent in care,
You left us forsaken, a world stripped bare.

Alone we stand, shattered and forlorn,
Lost in the void, hearts turned to stone.
You've led us astray, deserted and cold,
In your absence, the truth takes hold.

Nowhere to turn, lost in the night,
Beneath the moon's glow, seeking insight.
Was standing alone, gazing at the celestial rhyme,
Breeze brushed my soul, a fleeting moment in time.

~Kumar Patel and Srushti Pandey

19. Echoes of a Silent Love

Was once beautiful,
Was once horrible.
Love taught me how to breathe,
Then left me gasping for air.

The scent of your cologne—
a ghost of warmth I'll never hold.
The wind that whispered your name,
now just a bitter breeze in the cold.

Your touch, once familiar,
now fades into the shadows—
that hair I used to touch,
now nothing but a memory that gnaws.

Memories that no longer dare to show themselves,
Yet they haunt my soul,
alive in the spaces I cannot reach.
A past that refuses to leave.

If I could hold your hand again,
tell you that I still fall,
even as I drown in your absence,
I would.

But your eyes—
they stare back at me,
empty and cold,
like a dead sea,
and I am lost in its depths.

I see a stranger now—
a shell of a person,
alive in body,
but their soul has long been erased.
What once was warmth,
now churns like black water—
stirred, dark, and unforgiving.

Let me call this the end—
I don't need closure,
just silence.
All I see is an ocean of void,
a sea where hope drowned.

I'll keep this love buried inside me,
in a place no one will touch,
and let the winds of time
carry the grief far away.

Her broken heart is searching,
not for love,

but for a reason to breathe again—
to find a hand that will not vanish
when the dark clouds arrive.
It knows that eventually,
it will be whole,
but only if the hope that once lived within it
can be resurrected from the ashes.

Until then,
I am lost.
My heart, a graveyard
of promises unkept.
I still wait for you—
but you are a ghost,
and ghosts never return

20. When Two Worlds Almost Met

He

He never thought he'd change for anyone.
Not even for the ones who raised him.
But for her —
he changed without even realizing it.

He began to heal the broken pieces he used to hide.
Started standing taller, speaking softer, thinking wiser.
He started to care —
about himself,
about the life he was building,
because for the first time, someone made him believe he
was capable of more.

He stopped wasting time on empty dreams.
He started fixing routines he once laughed at.
Started waking up early, dressing better, eating healthier,
working harder.

He wanted to be the man she could proudly call hers.
Not just a boy floating through life —
but a man who could be her shelter when the world

grew cold.

For him, she wasn't a passing crush.
She was the wish he never said out loud,
the prayer whispered at 2AM when loneliness felt too
big.

She saw him.
She encouraged him.
She complimented him —
and that was all it took for him to build a whole future
around her.

He didn't just want to love her.
He wanted to grow with her —
career-wise, emotionally, financially —
in every way a man dreams of when he stops being a
boy.

For him,
she wasn't just *someone*.
She was *the one*.

.

She

She had spent years searching for someone real.
Someone who felt like home,

someone whose presence didn't need to be loud to be
felt.

And then he arrived.
Like a storm wrapped in calmness.
A friend who made her laugh louder,
feel safer,
smile wider.

He listened to her like no one ever did.
He remembered the tiny things she thought didn't
matter.
He showed up —
not with grand gestures,
but in the ways that truly mattered.

And somehow,
he became a part of her life without even knocking.
Without even asking.

She would laugh at herself sometimes —
Why has he become part of my routine?
Why do I shift my world just to hear him talk?
Why does it feel like I met him months ago, but my heart
insists it's been years?

There was something pure between them.

Something sacred.
A bond that felt like a rare thread in a world of loose
ends.

She convinced herself it was just friendship.
Because friendship was safer.
Because love —
love could tear things apart.

And she loved him —
as a friend.
Or so she told herself.
Over and over again.

Two people —
both feeling,
both hoping,
both terrified to name it.
He loved her like she was his future.
She loved him like he was her safest place.

They lived in two different worlds,
even though their souls sat side by side.

And that's how it goes, doesn't it?
Two people finding in each other what they searched for
all their lives —

but choosing silence over risk.
Calling it friendship instead of love.
Holding back because fear screamed louder than their
hearts.

And the world spins on.
Unaware of two people
who almost, almost had everything.

21. The Funeral of Our Hands

We met like rivers crashing into each other —
full, wild, ready to give everything.
You held my broken pieces like they were sacred,
and I cupped your fears like they were flowers.

We didn't know how to take,
only how to pour.
And so we kept pouring,
and pouring,
and pouring —
until our hands were empty,
but our hearts still begged for more.

You gave in the way you knew —
you fixed, you protected, you stayed.
I gave in the way I knew —
I softened, I listened, I disappeared.

Two givers,
both so desperate to heal the other,
we forgot we were bleeding too.

At first, it was beautiful —

the way we stitched our wounds with each other's
laughter,
the way we built shelters inside our bruised ribs.
We called it love,
we wore it like armor against a world that never stayed.

But the truth about givers is —
they pour even from an empty cup.
They promise even when their voice shakes.
They love until their hands tremble from holding too
much.

You gave until you forgot how to need.
I gave until I forgot how to ask.
You lost yourself trying to be enough for me.
I lost myself trying not to be a burden for you.

We were two oceans,
each trying to drown ourselves
so the other could float.

And slowly, without noticing,
we began to erode.
Tired smiles.
Silent dinners.
Hollow promises whispered like prayers neither of us
believed anymore.

Until one day —
without anger,
without betrayal,
without even a goodbye —
we ended.

Not because we stopped loving.
But because we never learned how to be loved.

You —
the boy who only knew how to give,
even when he was empty.
Me —
the girl who only knew how to unlove herself,
even when all she wanted was to be held.

We broke —
quietly,
painfully,
honestly.

Two givers —
who touched souls,
but couldn't stay whole.

And somewhere, in another life,

maybe we are still holding hands,
still saving each other,
still laughing without the fear of breaking.

But here, in this brutal, beautiful life,
we loved ourselves empty,
and walked away —
aching,
grateful,
forever unfinished.

Because not every story ends with goodbye.
Some stories end because two hearts
could not learn how to be full
without first learning how to take.

Epilogue — "The Graveyard of Givers"

In the end, two givers didn't shatter in anger.

They simply rotted in silence.

*They gave, and gave, and gave — until there was
nothing left to bury but the bones of who they used
to be.*

And when they finally let go...

it wasn't goodbye.

It was two empty hands brushing against each other one last time,

too tired to even hold on.

www.ingramcontent.com/pod-product-compliance
Lightning Source LLC
La Vergne TN
LVHW050929200726

843508LV00011B/2295